Rough Guides

25 Ultimate experiences

France

Make the most of your time on Earth

5.99

ROUGH GUIDES

25 YEARS 1982–2007

NEW YORK • LONDON • DELHI

Contents

Introduction

EXPERIENCES have always been at the heart of the Rough Guide concept. A group of us began writing the books **25 years ago** (hence this celebratory mini series) and wanted to share the kind of travels we had been doing ourselves. It seems bizarre to recall that in the early 1980s, travel was very much a minority pursuit. Sure, there was a lot of tourism around, and that was reflected in the guidebooks in print, which traipsed around the established sights with scarcely a backward look at the local population and their life. We wanted to change all that: to put a country or a city's popular culture centre stage, to highlight the clubs where you could hear local music, drink with people you hadn't come on holiday with, watch the local football, join in with the festivals. And of course we wanted to push travel a bit further, inspire readers with the confidence and knowledge to break away from established routes, to find pleasure and excitement in remote islands, or desert routes, or mountain treks, or in street culture.

Twenty-five years on, that thinking seems pretty obvious: we all want to experience something real about a destination, and to seek out travel's **ultimate experiences**. Which is exactly where these **25 books** come in. They are not in any sense a new series of guidebooks. We're happy with the series that we already have in print. Instead, the **25s** are a collection of ideas, enthusiasms and inspirations: a selection of the very best things to see or do – and not just before you die, but now. Each selection is gold dust. That's the brief to our writers: there is no room here for the average, no space fillers. Pick any one of our selections and you will enrich your travelling life.

But first of all, take the time to browse. Grab a half dozen of these books and let the ideas percolate ... and then begin making your plans.

Mark Ellingham
Founder & Series Editor, Rough Guides

25

Ultimate
experiences
France

01
Lording it in the Loire

You can't translate the word château. "Castle" is too warlike, "palace" too regal – and besides, they're all so different: some are grim and broken keeps, others lofty Gothic castles or exquisite Renaissance manor houses. Many are elegant country residences whose tall, shuttered windows overlook sweeps of rolling parkland. And a few – the finest – are magnificent royal jewels set in acre upon acre of prime hunting forest.

Today, the aristocracy no longer lord it over every last village in France, but a surprising number still cling to their ancestral homes. Some eke out a living offering tours, and the most fascinating châteaux are not always the greatest palaces but the half-decrepit country homes of faded aristocrats who will show off every stick of furniture, or tell you stories of their ancestors in the very chapel where they themselves will one day be buried.

Some owners, enticingly, even offer bed and breakfast. You get a vividly personal sense of France's patrician past when you wake up and see the moonlight shining through the curtains of your original, seventeenth-century four-poster – as at the château de Brissac in Anjou. Or when you gaze from your leaded window down an ancient forest ride in the Manoir de la Renomonière in Touraine, or draw a chair up to the giant stone bedroom fireplace at the perfectly tumbledown château de Chémery, near Blois.

As for the great royal residences, most are now cold and empty. National monuments like Chambord, a "hunting lodge" with a chimney for every day of the year, or Fontainebleau, where the Mona Lisa once hung in the royal bathroom, are the stunning but faded fruits of a noble culture that cherished excellence and had the money to pay for it in spades. But thanks to the tourist trade, many châteaux are recovering their former glory. The French state now scours auction houses all over the world for the fine furnishings flogged off by the wagon-load after the Revolution. Once empty and echoing, the royal palaces will soon be gilded once more – if not, perhaps, occupied.

need to know
Château de Brissac, Brissac-Quincé (☎ 02.41.91.22.21, ⓦ www.chateau-brissac.fr); Château de Chémery, Loir-et-Cher (☎ 02.54.71.82.77, ⓔ chateaudechemery @wanadoo.fr); Manoir de la Rémonière, near Azay-le-Rideau (☎ 02.47.45.24.88, ⓦ www .manoirdelaremoniere.com).

9

02

Swimming under the **Pont du Gard**

*A*monumentally graceful section of the Roman aqueduct that once supplied Nîmes with fresh water, the Pont du Gard is an iconic structure, a tribute both to the engineering prowess of its creators and, with its lofty, elegant triple-tiered arches, to their aesthetic sensibilities. Though mostly long-gone today, the aqueduct originally cut boldly through the countryside for a staggering 50km, across hills, through a tunnel and over rivers. The bridge has endured, though, providing inspiration for the masons and architects who, over the centuries, travelled from all over France to see it, meticulously carving their names and home towns into the weathered, pale gold stone.

A fancy visitor centre gives you the lowdown on the construction of the bridge, but a better way to get up close and personal to this architectural marvel is to follow the hundreds of French visitors who descend on a sunny day: make for the rocky banks of the River Gard, don your swimming things and take to the water. The tiers of arches rise high above you and to either side, with just one of the six lower arches making a superbly confident step across the river. Propelled by the gentle current of the reassuringly shallow Gard, you can float right under the arch, which casts a dense shadow onto the turquoise water. Beyond the bridge the river widens, and fearless kids leap from the rocks adjoining the aqueduct into the deepening waters, while families tuck into lavish picnics on the banks.

The splendour of the Pont du Gard made eighteenth-century philosopher and aqueduct enthusiast Rousseau wish he'd been born a Roman – perhaps he chose to ignore the fact that the bridge was built by slave labour. Better to be a twenty-first-century visitor – the only labour you'll have to expend is a bit of backstroke as you look up at what is still, after 2000 years, one of France's most imposing monuments.

need to know

The Pont du Gard is 8km from Uzès, from where there are frequent shuttle buses. For more information, visit ⓦwww.pontdugard.fr.

03 *Washing it down*
WITH CIDER IN NORMANDY

Normandy is to cider what Bordeaux is to wine. Sparkling, crisp and refreshing, it's the perfect foil to the artery-clogging food that Normans also do rather well – and as some of France's best food and drink comes from the rolling hills and green meadows of Normandy's Pays d'Auge, dining at a country restaurant in these parts is an experience not to miss.

The bottle of cider plonked down by your waiter may look as distinguished as a fine champagne, but don't stand on ceremony: open it quickly and take a good swig while it's still cold.

Norman cider is typically sweeter and less alcoholic than its English cousin, but it's the invigorating fizz which tickles the back of the throat and bubbles up through the nose that you'll remember.

You could try a *kir normand*: cider mixed with cassis – a more sophisticated and much more delicious French take on that old student favourite, "snakebite and black".

Make sure that you have a full glass ready for the arrival of your *andouilles* starter: although it won't necessarily enhance the taste of assorted blood and guts in a sausage, a generous gulp of cider will help get it down. Pork and cider, on the other hand, is one of the classic combinations of Norman cooking. Opt for some pork chops to follow and they come drowned in a thick, deliciously satisfying sauce with as much cream in it as cider. At this point, you may be offered the *trou normand*: a shot of Calvados apple brandy that helps digestion, apparently by lighting a fire in the pit of your stomach that burns through even the toughest *andouilles*' intestines. The *trou* clears just enough room for a slice of Camembert or Pont-l'Evêque, two of the famous cheeses produced in the Pays d'Auge, before you can finally leave the table, full and just a bit wobbly.

need to know
The Route du Cidre is a 40km loop linking the main cider-producing villages in the Pays d'Auge. The best cider makers display a "Cru de Cambremer" sign outside their farms, and many offer guided tours and free tastings. For more information, visit ⓦ www.calvados-tourisme.com.

4

Climbing the
Mont St-Michel

Wondrously unique yet as recognizable as the Eiffel Tower, Mont St-Michel and its harmonious blend of natural and man-made beauty has been drawing tourists and pilgrims alike to the Normandy coast for centuries. Rising some eighty metres from the waters of the bay that bears its name, this glowering granite outcrop has an entire commune clinging improbably to its steep boulders, its tiers of buildings topped by a magnificent Benedictine abbey.

From a few kilometres away, the sheer scale of the Mont provides an almost surreal backdrop to the rural tranquillity of Normandy – a startling welcome for the first-time visitor. And as you approach along the causeway that connects the Mont to the rest of France, the grandeur of this World Heritage Site becomes all the more apparent. Up close, the narrow, steepening streets offer an architectural history lesson, with Romanesque and Gothic buildings seemingly built one on top of the

Perched at the summit is the abbey itself, gushingly described by Guy de Maupassant as "the most wonderful Gothic building ever made for God on this earth". Although the first church was founded here in 709, today's abbey was constructed between the eleventh and thirteenth centuries, under Norman and subsequently French patronage. And as much as it's an aesthetic delight, the abbey is also a place of serenity: less than a third of the 3.5 million tourists that flock here each year actually climb all the way up to see it, and it remains a perfect place to be still and contemplate the Mont's glorious isolation.

Looking out from Mont St-Michel, as you watch the tides rolling in around its base – "like a galloping horse", said Victor Hugo – you can understand why medieval pilgrims would risk drowning to reach it, and why no invading force has ever succeeded in capturing the rock. It's a panorama to be savoured – as fine a sight as that of the Mont itself, and one that'll stay with you for a long time.

need to know

Buses to Mont-St-Michel leave from the train stations at Pontorson, St-Malo and Rennes. It's free to access the Mont but parking on the island or connecting causeway is €4. Further details can be found at ⓦwww .ot-montsaintmichel.com.

05

A SIP OF SUNLIGHT: WINE-TASTING IN *Bordeaux*

Margaux, Pauillac, Sauternes, St-Emilion – some of the world's most famous wines come from the vineyards encircling Bordeaux. So famous, in fact, that until recently, most châteaux didn't bother about marketing their wares. But times are changing: faced with greater competition and falling demand, more and more are opening their doors to the public. It's never been easier to visit these châteaux and sample the wines aptly described as "bottled sunlight".

Ranging from top-rank names such as Mouton-Rothschild and Palmer to small, family-run concerns, there are plenty to choose from. Some make their wine according to time-honoured techniques; others are ultra high-tech, with gleaming, computer-controlled vats and automated bottling lines – and there's a growing number of organic producers, too. All are equally rewarding. During the visit you'll learn about soil types and grape varieties, about fermentation, clarification and the long, complicated process which transforms grapes into wine.

Though you rarely get to see inside the châteaux themselves, several offer other attractions to draw in the punters, from wine or wine-related museums to introductory wine-tasting classes (this being France, you can sometimes sign up children for the latter, too). And because not everyone is just here for the wine, there are also art galleries, sculpture parks, hot-air balloon trips and, around St-Emilion, underground quarries to explore.

All visits, nevertheless, end in the tasting room. In top-rank châteaux, an almost reverential hush descends as the bottles are lovingly poured out. The aficionados swirl glasses and sniff the aromas, take a sip, savour it and then spit it out. If you feel like it, an appreciative nod not always goes down well. And often, you will feel like it – because despite all the detailed scientific explanations of how they're produced, the taste of these wines suggests that magic still plays a part.

need to know

Local tourist offices and Maisons du Vin provide lists of producers offering vineyard visits. Most visits are free, though more famous châteaux may charge up to €8. It's always best to phone ahead, especially off-season or if you'd like an English-speaking guide.

06 Paying your respects in Normandy

Apart from the German stronghold of Pointe du Hoc, where gleeful kids take time out from building sandcastles to clamber over the rubble of battered bunkers, the D-Day landing beaches – Sword, Juno, Gold, Omaha and Utah – contain few physical traces of their bloody past. It's almost as though the cheery banality of summertime in the seaside towns along this stretch of the Norman coast has grown like poppies over the painful memories of June 6, 1944. The beaches are dotted with gaily painted wooden bathing huts; the odd windsurfer braves the choppy grey-green waters; walkers ramble along the dunes; families up from Paris eat *moules frites* at beachside terraces – all a far cry from the horrible reality of the past, as re-enacted in the shocking opening scene of *Saving Private Ryan*.

But while the sands are consumed by summer's frivolity, the cemeteries built to bury the D-Day dead serve as sanctuaries for those who don't want to forget. People shuffle in silence across the well-manicured lawns of the American burial ground on a cliff overlooking Omaha, where rows of perfectly aligned white crosses sweep down to the cliff's edge and appear to continue for miles into the sea. In the church-like peace and tranquillity, broken only by the sharp cries of seagulls, uniformed veterans remember fallen comrades and families lost husbands and fathers. Even the children, too young to even understand the sacrifices made, are humbled by the solemnity of their surroundings, affording only glancing and indifferent looks at the kites swirling in the breeze before returning to the poignantly simple white crosses that have made the grown-ups so quiet.

need to know

The Normandy landing beaches stretch west from the mouth of the River Orne near Caen to the Cotentin Peninsula south of Cherbourg. Informative tours of the landing beaches are offered by the Caen Memorial (🖥 www.memorial-caen.fr).

07 Macaroons fit for a Monarch

It's **5.30pm** on a Friday, and a queue stretches out through the door of Ladurée, on rue Royale near the place de la Madeleine. If you're wondering what the fuss is about, just take one look at the display of fabulous cakes and pastries inside – so renowned are Ladurée's confections that foodies will cross Paris for them and patiently wait their turn to have their purchases packed into elegant boxes.

If you feel you've earned yourself a sightseeing break, you could bypass the queue and head for the adjoining *salon de thé* or tea room, though the English translation hardly does justice to this luxurious parlour dating from 1862, decorated with gilt-edged mirrors, marble-topped tables and ceiling frescoes.

Once you're installed at your table, surrounded by elegantly coiffed *grandes dames* sporting Hermès scarves and fashionistas flanked by designer bags, a waitress in a long polka-dotted apron will take your order and flash you a complicitous look as you name your desired confection. You could let yourself be tempted by any number of heavenly gateaux, but if you've never tasted them, it's Ladurée's famous *macarons* (macaroons) that you should try. Nothing like the stodgy coconut-heavy cookies that you may know from back home, these are delicate almondy biscuits with a delicious ganache filling – at once crunchy and gooey. They come in a variety of flavours and pastel colours – the chocolate and blackcurrant are the best – and, like designer fashion collections, new flavours are launched each season.

More extravagant creations are also available, such as the *saint-honoré rose-framboise*; made of choux pastry, chantilly, raspberry compote and raspberries, and topped off with a rose petal, it has all the flouncy frou-frou of a dress from the court of Versailles. Perhaps unsurprising, then, that Ladurée was appointed the official *patissier* for Sofia Coppola's film, *Marie Antoinette*. "Let them eat cake!", wasn't the French queen supposed to have said? When the cakes are this good, it's hard to imagine why you'd want to eat anything else.

need to know
Ladurée (Mon–Sat 8.30am–7pm, Sun 10am–7pm; ⊛ www.laduree. fr) is at 16 rue Royale, and also has branches on the Champs-Elysées and rue Bonaparte.

08
BRAVING THE ELEMENTS
on the Brittany coast

need to know
Ferries from Portsmouth and Weymouth serve St-Malo on Brittany's northern coast, while Plymouth, Cork and Rosslare have services to Roscoff, about 175km west of St-Malo in Finistère. Southwest of Roscoff, Pointe du Raz occupies the westernmost tip of Finistère (and Brittany). For more information on Brittany, visit Ⓦ www .brittanytourism.com.

There's no better place to prepare for Brittany's wild and ragged coast than St-Malo. Fresh off the ferry from England, it's easy to imagine that you've been transported back to a time when pirates drank in the taverns and swaggered through the cobbled streets of the old citadel. Head up onto the ramparts and you'll hear the angry sea seething below and feel drops of water smack against your face as a black cloud passes overhead on its way down the Breton coast towards Finistère.

With a name that translates as "the end of the world", Finistère is one of the most isolated parts of France. Its bleak and beautiful sense of loneliness hits you with every gust of wind that blows in off the sea and sweeps across the heather-covered headlands, ruffling your hair, watering your eyes and filling your lungs with fresh, moist air. Roscoff, Finistère's second-largest port, looks like a sleepy outpost compared with St-Malo's swashbuckling citadel, its forlorn fishing boats stuck in the mud at low tide and shafts of light piercing through dark clouds that forever threaten rain.

Southeast of Roscoff, and marking Finistère's (and France's) Land's End, Pointe du Raz is one of Brittany's busiest attractions. But even though a million people visit each year, you don't have to walk for too long before the windswept paths that weave precariously around the promontory become deserted, and it's just you and the ocean. Only this time, the sea that bubbled beneath St-Malo's ramparts is now crashing ferociously against the precipitous cliffs that bring France to such a sudden and dramatic end. "In chasmal beauty looms that wild weird western shore", wrote Thomas Hardy of the Cornish cliffs across the Channel, but his inspiration could just as easily have come from this powerful and strangely seductive swathe of coastline.

Partying the night away at a

Summer fête

Catching a village fête is more down to serendipity than planning. A tiny poster in the local boulangerie or boucherie might be the only sign that something's afoot, but don't let rural France's publicity deficiencies put you off. All and sundry are welcome at the annual alfresco parties hosted by each commune; just turn up, dust off your beginners' French and prepare for something infinitely more absorbing than the minor soirée suggested by the posters. Returning to the village on fête night is often like being transported to a different planet: market stalls are packed away, and people from neighbouring towns spill out of once-sleepy bars whose evening clientele usually only numbers the barman and a sole farmer nursing a cognac.

Trestle tables groaning with delicacies are set up around the square, jealously presided over by the village grand-mères. Faddy eaters would be advised to ensure that their personal bête-noire foodstuff doesn't coincide with the local specialities that inevitably dominate the menu: intestine-filled *andouillette* sausages in the north, perhaps, or salads sprinkled with *gésiers* (goose gizzards), and *tripoux* – sheep's stomach stuffed with tripe, trotters, pork and garlic – in the Dordogne and Lot. Most offerings are delicious, but if you do encounter something that offends your palate, it can at least be washed down with a couple of glasses of vin de table – which tastes a whole lot better in the open air than it should, particularly when drunk from plastic pint glasses.

Later in the evening, "le rock" bands pour their music into the darkening air and the strings of lights decorating the trees provide a sparkly, festive air. Street performers wander and, as the sun finally sets, everyone gets down to some serious wine consumption and dancing. The sight of the village elders and teenagers dancing together to slightly dubious French bands on hastily erected stages may seem incongruous, but only serves to reinforce the nagging feeling that everything is somehow more civilized in France.

need to know

Village festivals and celebrations are held the length and breadth of France throughout the year, although the summer usually brings a glut. There's usually no entry fee, but there tends to be a small charge for food and drink – ten euros or so will see you fed and watered all night.

shaken and stirred
in Monte-Carlo

There are lots of casinos along the French Riviera, but only one Casino de Monte-Carlo. The Lilliputian royal palace of the ruling Grimaldi family may be the official heart of Monaco, but in splendour and fame it's quite outgunned by the Casino de Monte-Carlo, easily the world's most historic and magnificent homage to gambling.

Well into the twentieth century, it was the Casino's coffers that kept the precarious little statelet of Monaco financially viable, and it was the Casino that made the Grimaldis glamorous enough to marry into Hollywood royalty in 1956, when Prince Rainier wed ice-cool Grace Kelly.

The building glitters and sparkles in the Mediterranean sunshine like the belle époque jewel it is; the architect, Charles Garnier, also designed the Paris opera house, and was not a man to leave any stone unturned – or any rocaille ungilded – in his quest for showy magnificence. Once inside, you show your ID and check in coats and bags – and if your clothing is deemed inappropriate, you won't get any further. But this isn't a place to visit in beachwear, anyway: better to wear your finest and wander its salons with Bond-like insouciance. At certain times, your entrance fee will be reimbursed in chips for the tables, which is enough to make even the most sceptical of visitors feel part of the action.

Most go no further than the Salons Europe, the first in a series of increasingly discreet and opulent rooms leading from the grand lobby which culminate in the inner sanctum of the Salons Privés.

But even the Salons Europe have a certain mystique. Despite the incongruous ranks of bleeping, flashing slot machines, it's the roulette table that takes centre stage. Sombre, serious and more than a little obsessive, the faces of the serious gamblers around the table betray intense concentration. Hard though it is to banish thoughts of Ian Fleming's fictional alter ego, few real gamblers bear much resemblance to 007. Lately, they've built a Monte Carlo Resort and Casino in Las Vegas. But Monaco's jewel remains the real *Casino Royale.*

need to know

The Casino de Monte-Carlo (@www.casinomontecarlo.com), Place du Casino, is open daily to visitors aged 18 and over from noon. You'll pay €10 for entry to the Salons Europe, and €20 for the Salons Privés, which open at 4pm.

11

Castles in the Sky

The Cathar strongholds
of Languedoc-Roussillon

It's hard to forget the first time you catch a glimpse of the Château de Peyrepertuse. In fact, it takes a while before you realize that this really is a castle, not just some fantastic rock formation sprouting from the mountain top. But it's no mirage – 800 years ago, men really did haul slabs of stone up here to build one of the most hauntingly beautiful fortresses in Europe.

In medieval France, war was frequent, life often violent – the point of castles, obviously enough, was to provide a degree of protection from all of that. Location was all-important –and the Cathar lords of Languedoc-Roussillon took this to ludicrous extremes, building them in seemingly impossible places. How they even laid foundations boggles the mind. Approach Peyrepertuse on foot, from the village of Duilhac, and you'll soon see why. Improbably perched on the edge of long, rocky ridge, it's surrounded by a sheer drop of several hundred metres, and its outer walls cleverly follow the contours of the mountain, snaking around the summit like a stone viper. Inside, at the lower end, is the main keep, a solid grey cube of rock that looks like it could withstand a battering from smart bombs, never mind medieval

cannon. But to really appreciate the fortress, you have to get closer.

It's a sweaty hour-long hike to the top, but when you clamber through the main entrance and onto the upper keep, the views from the battlements are stupendous: here, where the mountain ends in a vast, jagged stub of granite, there are no walls – you'd need wings to attack from this side.

Ironically, even castles like this couldn't protect the Cathars. In the early thirteenth century, this Christian cult was virtually exterminated after forty years of war and a series of massacres that were brutal even by medieval standards. Peyrepertuse was surrendered in 1240, but the fact that it still survives, as impressive now as it must have been centuries ago, is testament both to the Cathars' ingenious building skills and their passionate struggle for freedom.

need to know

The Château de Peyrepertuse sits above the village of Duilhac, around 25km from Perpignan in Languedoc-Roussillon (daily: Feb, March, Nov & Dec 10am–5pm; April, May and Oct 10am–6.30pm; June & Sept 9am–7pm; July & Aug 9am–8.30pm; €5; ⓦ www .chateau-peyrepertuse.com).

12

GRAND IMPRESSIONS
ON THE ART TRAIL IN THE CÔTE D'AZUR

Like most of Renoir's work, it's instantly appealing, with a dazzling range of colour and a warmth that radiates out from the canvas. A hazy farmhouse at the end of a driveway, framed by leafy trees and bathed in sunny pastel tones, *La Ferme des Collettes* is one of the artist's most famous paintings, perfectly evoking a hot, balmy day in the south of France.

But what makes this watercolour extra special is its location: it's one of eleven on show in the actual *ferme* depicted in the painting, a mansion in Cagnes-sur-Mer where the celebrated Impressionist lived and worked from 1907 until his death, and which is now the Musée Renoir. Step outside and you step right into the picture, bathed in the same bright light and warm Mediterranean air.

Ever since *pointillist* Paul Signac beached his yacht at St-Tropez in the 1880s, the Côte d'Azur has inspired more writers, sculptors and painters than almost anywhere on the planet. If you want to follow in their footsteps, Nice is the place to start, home to Henri Matisse for much of his life. Resist the temptations of the palm-fringed promenade and head inland to the Musée Matisse, a striking maroon-toned building set in the heart of an olive grove. Among the exotic works on display, *Nature morte aux grenades* offers a particularly powerful insight into the intense emotional connection Matisse established with this part of France, his vibrant use of raw, bold colour contrasting beautifully with the rough, almost clumsy style.

And then there's Picasso. Probably the greatest painter of the twentieth century, he spent a prolific year at the Château Grimaldi in Antibes, a short drive south of Nice. Now the Musée Picasso, it's packed with work from that period – the creative energy of *Ulysses and his Sirens*, a four metre-high representation of the Greek hero tied to the mast of his ship, is simply overwhelming. But it's hard to stare at something this intense for long, and you'll soon find yourself drifting to the windows – and the same spectacular view of the Mediterranean that inspired Picasso sixty years ago.

need to know
For more on the museums above, visit Ⓦ www.chez.com/renoir/cagnes.htm; Ⓦ www.musee-matisse-nice.org; or Ⓦ www.antibes-juanlespins.com/fr/culture/musees/picasso.

31

13 The Cocktail Crawl:
Bar Hopping in the MARAIS

Glaces et Sorbets de la Maison Berthillon

La Brasserie de l'Isle Saint Louis

It's 10pm and in bistros and restaurants all over Paris, diners are sipping coffee and draining the last drops of wine from their glasses. It's Saturday night, and time to hit the bars: perhaps the studenty haunts of the Left Bank, the glamorous see-and-be-seen places around the Champs-Elysées or the more bohemian, cutting-edge drinking dens in the east. But for style and sophistication, it's hard to beat the Marais, one of the most seductive areas of central Paris, full of splendid Renaissance mansions, narrow lanes and buzzing cafés and bars attracting a hip crowd that includes a strong gay contingent.

First stop might be a bustling champagne bar, where the waiter leads you up a narrow flight of winding stairs to the second and then third floor of a tall, thin building packed with cool young Parisians chattering away over bubbling flutes. But when there are so many different corners to explore, it's impossible to stay in one place for long, and you head back onto the streets as the intrigue of exploration takes hold.

The night passes in a blur of gin fizz cocktails, shouted conversations and impromptu dancing in a dazzling array of bars: a Moroccan den done up in sumptuous fabrics, where patrons puff on fragrant sheesha pipes; a retro joint where hipsters in fedoras and full skirts jockey for seats on mismatched salvaged chairs; a hardcore drinking hole where heavily muscled, black leather-clad men posture and preen; and a dark, sexy cocktail lounge with a soundtrack of cool, smooth jazz.

Stumble homeward in the wee hours, and you won't be able to resist making one last stop – it might turn out to be the find of the night, after all.

need to know

The Marais is right in the centre of Paris and comprises the €3 and €4 arrondissements; convenient Metro stations are Hotel de Ville, Rambuteau and St Paul. Classic bar-crawl stopoffs might include Andy Wahloo, 69 rue des Gravilliers; Lizard Lounge, 81 rue du Bourg-Tibourg; Guillame, 32 rue de Picardie; Les Bains, 7 rue du Bourg L'Abbél; and Chez Richard, 37 rue Vieille du Temple.

33

SEEING THE LIGHT
Prehistoric cave art at Pech-Merle

need to know
Grotte de Pech-Merle (mid-Jan to March and Nov to mid-Dec by group reservation only; April–Oct daily 9.30am–noon & 1.30–5pm; €7 mid-June to mid-Sept, rest of year €6; @www.quercy .net/pechmerle) is two hours' drive north of Toulouse. Tours are conducted in French, but an English guidebook is available.

Imagine a cave in total darkness. Then a tiny flame from a tar torch appears, piercing the blackness, and a small party of men carrying ochre pigment and charcoal crawl through the labyrinth. They select a spot on the cold, damp walls and start to paint, using nothing but their hands and a vivid imagination. Finished, they gather their torches and leave their work to the dark.

Until now. A mind-blowing 25,000 years later, you can stand in the Grotte de Pech-Merle and admire this same astonishing painting: two horses, the right-hand figure with a bold, naturalistic outline that contrasts with the decidedly abstract black dots – 200 of them – that fill up its body and surround the head. The whole thing is circled, enigmatically, by six handprints, while a red fish positioned above its back adds to the sense of the surreal.

Short of inventing a time machine, this is the closest you'll get to the mind of Stone Age man. And it's this intimacy, enhanced by the cool dimness of the cave, that makes a visit here so overwhelming. Unlike Lascaux in the Dordogne, Pech-Merle allows visitors to view the original art, and the so-called dotted horses are just the best-known of the cave's mesmerizing ensemble of 700 paintings, finger drawings and engravings of bison, mammoths and horses.

It was once common to think of prehistoric peoples as brutish, shaggy-haired cavemen waving clubs, but some 30,000 years ago here in France, they were busy creating the world's first naturalistic and abstract art. No one's sure just why they made these paintings, but it's possible that the tranquil, womb-like caves were sacred places linked to fertility cults, the drawings divided into male and female symbols suffused with Paleolithic mythology. But new theories suggest something far more prosaic: that the paintings were made primarily by teenage boys who had the subjects of hunting and women foremost on their minds. Perhaps Pech-Merle's most poignant treasure backs this up – the foot print of an adolescent boy, captured in clay as he left the cave one evening, some 25,000 years ago.

15 Deluxe dining in PARIS

Sumptuous decor, exquisite food, service that purrs along like a Rolls Royce and a hint of the theatrical – **Lasserre** has all the ingredients of a classic haute cuisine restaurant.

The drama starts as soon as you arrive, a lift lined with deep-purple velvet delivers you into an opulent Neoclassical-style salon. Pillars and balustrades festooned with flowers form the backdrop to elegant tables laid with antique silver cruets and Meissen porcelain. The walls and drapes are decorated in rich reds and golds and the ceiling is painted with a whirl of sylphlike dancing women; a chandelier provides the central flourish.

Diners are greeted by the charming Monsieur Louis, who ha been at the restaurant for nearly forty years; very soon you're in th hands of a highly efficient and discreet corps of waiters in tails, anticipating your every need and unfailingly attentive – monsieur ha spilt a little potage on his silk tie? Not to worry, a deft hand is soon dabbing it away.

But it's the food that really takes centre stage. This is cuisine of the hautest kind, traditional rather than modern: rich sauces, foie gras, caviar and truffles. Each dish is prepared with consummate artistry, each mouthful exquisitely intense. You might start with the artichokes in a wine sauce with courgette flowers and broad beans in argan oil, while for mains you could plump for one of the restaurant's classic dishes, such as *canard á l'orange* or *pigeon André Malraux*, the latter named after the Resistance hero and writer who once lunched here almost daily.

Save room for the signature dessert, *timbale Elysée-Lasserre*, a sublime creation of ice-cream, strawberries and chantilly cream canopied with a lattice of caramelized sugar. And it goes without saying that the wine list is exceptional – Lasserre's cellar holds some 200,000 bottles, mostly from Burgundy and Bordeaux, and there are fifty champagnes to choose from.

need to know
Lasserre is at 17 Av Franklin Roosevelt, Paris (☎01.43.59.02.13, ⓦwww .restaurant-lasserre.com). Reckon on at least €120 per head at dinner, €75 for the lunchtime set menu; there's also a seven-course *menu dégustation* at €185; prices exclude wine. Men must wear a jacket and tie.

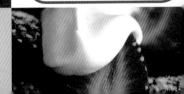

16
Going to the Medieval Movies

A world apart from piles of old stones, paintings of curly-wigged fat men or pungent-smelling chateaux, seeing the Bayeux Tapestry is more like going to the movies than trotting round a traditional tourist sight. Wrapped around a half-lit wall like a medieval IMAX theatre, it's protected by a glass case and dim lighting, while a deep, movie-trailer voice gives a blow-by-blow headphone commentary of the kings, shipwrecks and gory battles depicted in the comic-strip-like scenes.

The nuns who are thought to have embroidered this seventy-metre strip of linen with the story behind William of Normandy's conquest of England could hardly have guessed that, nearly a millennium later, people would be lining up to marvel at their meticulous artwork and impeccable storytelling.

But like Shakespeare's plays, the Bayeux Tapestry is one of history's timeless treasures. Okay, so the characters are two-dimensional, the ancient colours hardly HD and the scenes difficult to decipher without the commentary, but it's captivating nonetheless. William looks every bit the superhero on the back of his huge horse, while King Harold, with his dastardly moustache, appears the archetypal villain, his arrow in the eye a just dessert.

The wonderful detail adds intriguing layers to the main theme: the appearance of Halley's Comet as a bad omen when Harold is crowned king builds up the suspense, while the apparent barbecuing of kebabs on the beach has led some historians to argue that the tapestry is considerably newer than first thought. Whether this is true is of no great importance – the images are as engrossing now as they ever were, and on exiting the theatre, even the staunchest of Brits might feel enthused enough to be secretly pleased that a brave Frenchman crossed the Channel to give Harold his comeuppance. And in this way, the Bayeux Tapestry has lost none of its power as one of the finest pieces of propaganda the world has ever seen.

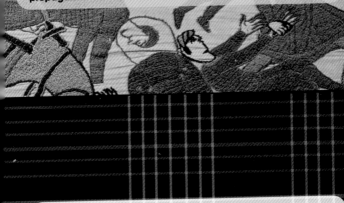

need to know
The tapestry is housed in the Centre Guillaume le Conquérant in Bayeux (daily: mid-March to April & Sept–Oct 9am–6.30pm; May–Aug 9am–7pm; Nov to mid-March 9.30am–12.30pm & 2–6pm; €7.60; ⓦ www.chateau-guillaume-leconquerant.fr).

17
Sloping off
to the FRENCH ALPS

Compared to the perfect, twinkling villages that abound in Austria, France's clunky, purpose-built ski resorts are distinctly lacking in poetry; and if you're after awesomely broad pistes and a beaming welcome, the US might be a better bet. But while no one country offers the perfect skiing experience, France does come pretty close.

From Chamonix's towering off-piste swells to Portes du Soliel's Swiss Wall, so steep that even the piste-bashing machines can't get down it, France has enough of the tough stuff to keep the most hardcore skiers and boarders happy. Few things are as thrilling as shivering at the top of an icy pinnacle and realizing that – unless you want to spend the night there – the only way is down, pulling long carves through glistening snow, taking bumps and jumps on loose knees and grinning as the world rushes by.

Of course, you don't have to be a boy racer to enjoy the French Alps. There are gentle, rolling pistes aplenty, as well as restaurants doling out immense portions of melted raclette cheese to vin chaud-supping French scenesters who never seem to get their skis wet. And the epic scope of what's on offer here is continually inspiring: in Val Thorens, the Alps boast the highest resort in Europe; the many glaciers here mean you can ski year-round; and Les Trois Vallées offers the world's largest ski area.

And if the desire to leave the grubby, humdrum lower world behind is as central to skiing and snowboarding as the need for speed, this glorious scale makes the French Alps a splendid place to escape to. Most people who come here return again and again and, before too many seasons are up, find themselves swearing like a native, discovering an unforeseen affection for unflattering jumpsuits and slipping into the amorphous lift queues with proper Gallic carelessness.

need to know

France's skiing season runs from January to April – outside that you'll be taking a chance or will be restricted to glacier skiing. For more on winter sports, visit ⊛www.skifrance.fr.

18
Champagne tasting
Épernay

Champagne is an exclusive drink, in all senses of the word, what with its upmarket associations and the fact that it can be made only from the grapes grown in the Champagne region of northern France. The centre of champagne production is Épernay, a town that's made much of its association with the ultimate fizzy stuff, and where all the *maisons* of the well-known champagne brands are lined up along the appropriately named Avenue de Champagne.

   All of these champagne houses offer tours and tastings, and one of the best places to indulge is at the *maison* of Moët et Chandon, arguably the best-known brand in the world. The splendid, cathedral-like cellars afford suitable dignity to this most regal of drinks, while the multi-lingual guides explain the complexities of blending different grapes and vintages to maintain a consistency of flavour from one year to the next. During the tasting, an enthusiastic sommelier explains the subtleties of flavour in the different cuvées, and although the whole experience can feel rather impersonal, it's nonetheless an essential part of any visit to the region.

For an altogether more exclusive experience, head ten miles or so north of Épernay to the village of Bligny. Here, the eighteenth-century Chateau de Bligny is the only one in France still producing its own champagne and, if you call ahead, you can arrange a private tour. Driving through the wrought-iron gates and up the scrunchy gravel driveway, a sense of understated class strikes you immediately, and things only get classier as you're taken through the tastefully furnished rooms and vaulted cellars, and shown the family's cherished champagne flute collection. A tasting of several prize-winning vintages, taken in the opulent drawing room, is of course included, and as you savour your second glass of prize-winning bubbles, you'll doubtless conclude that there's no better place to get a flavour of the heady world of champagne than the home ground of this "drink of kings".

need to know

The Office de Tourisme, 7 Avenue de Champagne, Épernay (☎03.26.53.33.00, ⓦ www.ot-epernay.fr), has information on touring all the town's champagne houses. To organize a private tour of the Chateau de Bligny, call ☎03.25.27.40.11 well in advance.

We'd set out in pre-dawn darkness to ascend the spectacular head of the Vallée d'Asco, ringed by peaks nudging 3000m. High above, an enfolding wall of snow-streaked granite glowed crimson in the first rays of daylight. Small flocks of *mouflon* sheep were already grazing overhead, sending small pebbles spiralling down the cliffs as we began the first pass of the day.

The view from the col was astounding. Looking northwards along the serrated ridge-tops of the watershed, tiers of shadowy summits receded to a sea the colour of lapis. The light was exceptionally vivid all the way to the horizon, where a front of white cloud was floating above the French Riviera.

Except it wasn't cloud. As a glance through the binoculars confirmed, the white apparition in the distance was in fact the southern reaches of the Alps – a staggering 250km away. What we'd assumed was a small yacht on its way to St Tropez or Toulon was in fact a massive car ferry the size of a block of flats. The realization was overwhelming, completely overturning our sense of space and scale.

Seeing the Alps from such a distance may have been a one off, but every day on the GR20 – France's famous *haute route* across the Mediterranean island of Corsica – brings astonishing moments. The ingenious red-and-white waymarks lead you across terrain of incredible variety. On a typical *étape* you could climb passes nearly two-and-a-half kilometres high, picnic by frozen glacial lakes, skinny dip in mountain streams, skid down eternal snow patches and come face to face at the bottom a with wild boar.

Best of all, at the end of it, having hauled yourself through all fifteen *étapes*, you can rest your aching bones in the most translucent turquoise water in the entire Mediterranean

eed to know The GR20 is open from early June until mid-October. Most people need between 10 and 13 days to complete all 15 *étapes*. Accommodation along the way is provided by basic *refuges*, whose *gardiens* also sell provisions (at extortionate prices).

19

19,000m of knee-crunching climbs:

Hiking Corsica's
GR20

20

Mingling with Masters on the Left Bank

Impressionist paintings at the Musée d'Orsay

Forget the Louvre, it's not a patch on the Musée d'Orsay – or so you'll be told. Maybe this is down to continued bitterness toward futuristic glass pyramids, but it's probably more about the understated elegance of the Musée d'Orsay itself. Handsomely located in a renovated turn-of-the-century railway station, the museum's splendid collection of vibrant Impressionist canvases are displayed in much more intimate surrounds, right up under the roof in a wing whose attic-like feel is far less formal and imposing than the Louvre.

A wander through the compact Impressionist and Post-Impressionist galleries provides an astonishingly comprehensive tour of the best paintings of the period, the majority of them easily recognizable classics like Van Gogh's *Starry Night* or Renoir's *Dance at Le Moulin de la Galette*. Even better, these are paintings you can really engage with, their straightforward style and vibrant, life-like scenes drawing you into the stories they tell. It's easy to forget where you are and, transfixed, reach out a finger to trace the chunky swirls of paint that make up Van Gogh's manic skies; you might even catch yourself imitating the movements of Degas' delicate ballerinas as they dance across the walls, sweeping their arms in arcs above their heads and pointing their tiny toes.

When the intricate grandeur of Monet's *Rouen Cathedral* looms above you and reinstates a sense of decorum, it's almost as if you were standing under the imposing bulk of the old building itself. Exhilaration returns as you're transported to the tropics by Gauguin's disarming Tahitian maids, who eye you coyly from the depths of the jungle. But don't get so caught up in the stories that you forget the incredible artistic prowess on display; stick your nose right up to Seurat's dotted *Cirque*, then inch slowly backwards and, as the yellow-clad acrobats appear with their white horse, you'll feel the immense genius of the pioneer of pointillism.

need to know

On the Left Bank opposite the Tuileries gardens, the Musée d'Orsay's (ⓦwww .musee-orsay.fr) entrance is on Rue de la Légion d'Honneur. The nearest Metro is Solférino; Musée d'Orsay is the closest RER station.

Lunching in rural France

21

Expect to pay €15–25 for a four-course lunch in a traditional rural restaurant; this often includes wine and coffee.

Picture a village square with tables set out under ancient trees, and dappled sunlight playing on waiters bearing plates of local delicacies whose heady aromas fill the air. While this archetypal image of a restaurant in rural France is of course a cliché, such places do still exist – just ask around, or keep your eyes open as you drive through the villages. Then take your place at the table and give your tastebuds a treat.

The most traditional of rural restaurants won't offer a choice – you simply sit down and the food starts to arrive. To whet the appetite, you help yourself from a tureen of soup, one of those wonderful "everlasting" concoctions whose flavours become ever more complex by the day.

Depending on the region, your next course is likely to be a selection of charcuterie or crudités, a slice of savoury tart or perhaps mussels if you're near the coast. The main dish will almost always be meat: a juicy steak, a hearty beef or game stew, or maybe roast pork or lamb laced with herbs and a hefty dose of garlic. Though fried potatoes and green beans are the usual accompaniment, you may get something more interesting such as a vegetable gratin or fragrant wild mushrooms.

Then it's a green salad and the cheese board, hopefully a sampler of local specialities: soft, creamy rounds of Brie or Brillat-Savarin; aromatic, blue-veined wedges of Roquefort; and goats' cheese in herb-crusted pyramids. You're now on the home straight.

If space allows, dessert could be a simple sorbet or bowl of summer-sweet seasonal fruits, or a more elaborate confectionery such as *clafoutis* (upside-down cake), *croustade* (apple tart laced with armagnac) or the classic, totally irresistible chocolate mousse. No French meal is complete without a coffee – black and strong – and after such an extravaganza you may feel the need for a brandy or other digestif. Then it's time to pay up and find a shady spot for your siesta.

Cathédrale St-Etienne

A flat plain at the very heart of France, stranded between the verdant Loire valley and the abundant hillsides of Burgundy, the Berry region has become a byword for provincial obscurity. This really is *la France profonde*, the cherished "deep France", whose peasant traditions continue to resist the modernization that threatens – so they say – to engulf the nation. You can drive for miles here without seeing anything except open fields and modest farmhouses.

As you approach the miniature regional capital of Bourges, however, a mighty landmark begins to reveal itself. Looming over the fields, allotments and low houses is a vast Gothic cathedral, its perfect skeleton of flying buttresses and keel-like roof giving it the look of a huge ship in dry dock. A stupendous relic of the inexorable, withdrawing tide of power and belief, its preposterous size and wealth of detailing prove that the Berry was not always a backwater. In the early thirteenth century, when the cathedral was built, this was a powerful and wealthy region – and Bourges' archbishops wanted all the world to know it.

At the foot of the impossibly massive west front, five great portals yawn open, their deep arches fringed by sculptures. You could spend hours gazing at the central portal, which depicts the Last Judgement in appalling detail, complete with snake-tailed and wing-arsed devils, and damned souls – some wearing bishops' mitres – screaming from the bottom of boiling cauldrons.

Inside, the prevailing mood is one of quieter awe. The magnificent nave soars to an astonishing 38 metres, and is ringed by two tall aisles. No matter where you look, smooth-as-bone columns power their way from marble floor to tent-like vault, their pale stone magically dappled with colours cast by some of Europe's finest, oldest and deepest-hued stained glass. Behind the high altar, at the very heart of the cathedral and at the very centre of France, the apse holds these jewels of the Berry: precious panels of coloured glass, their images of the Crucifixion, the Last Judgement, the Apocalypse and of Joseph and his coat glowing like gemstones.

> ### need to know
> Entrance to the Cathédrale St-Etienne, place Etienne Dolet, is free (April–June & Sept 8.30am–7.15pm; July & Aug 8.30am–7.45pm; Oct–March 9am–5.45pm), but you can pay €5 to climb the tower, or €9 to descend into the crypt as well.

Feeding the SENSES at a Provençal market

Look at Van Gogh's sunflower paintings and you're struck first and foremost by their vivid colours. Vincent was living in Provence when he painted the most famous of this iconic series, and on a sun-drenched market-day morning in this part of France, you'll get an idea of just what inspired him.

The colours are magnificent: heaps of bold and brash yellows and oranges pile up against each other at a spice stand; bunches of asparagus look like Roman torches burning with deep purple flames; and you can almost see Van Gogh's brushstrokes in a peach's sensual wisps of red, crimson and pink.

But a painting can't convey the smells that infuse these colours with life. Sauntering from stall to stall, wafts of chives, lavender, olives and wild thyme combine to create one-of-a-kind olfactory tributes to the bewildering variety of produce that grows in the region.

23

And as you stroll through this gloriously technicoloured world, past tanned Mediterranean faces grinning behind stalls overflowing with produce fit for heaven, it's easy to believe that you're smack in the middle of one of Walt's more winsome movies and that Van Gogh's sunflowers are yours for a few euros a dozen.

Melons, cut into bite-sized tasting cubes, are seductively fragrant. The piscatorial ingredients of Marseille's famous bouillabaisse lie on a bed of ice, eyes bulging and smelling of the sea. And a hefty leg of ham at *Pascal's* butchers gives off a tangy aroma that turns your thoughts irresistibly to lunch. This is the type of romantic market scene that might be dreamed up for a feelgood Disney film.

need to know

Virtually every town in Provence holds a market at least once a week. Among the biggest are those in Aix-en-Provence (Sat; 9am–12.30pm) and Marseille (Sun; 8am–7pm).

24

Created around 3300 BC, Carnac's three alignments of over two thousand menhirs comprise the greatest concentration of standing stones in the world. Come here in the summer, and you'll encounter crowds and boundary ropes. But visit during the winter and you can wander among them freely – and if you arrive just after sunrise, when the mist still clings to the coast, you'll be accompanied by nothing but the birds and the sounds of the local farms waking up.

Just to the north of town, where the stones of the Le Ménec alignment are at their tallest, you can walk between broken megalithic walls that stand twice your height. Stretching for more than 100m from one side to the other and extending for over a kilometre, the rows of stones might first seem part of a vast art installation. Each is weathered and worn by five thousand years of Atlantic storms, and their stark individuality provides a compelling contrast to the symmetry of the overall arrangement. But it's hard to believe there wasn't something religious about them.

need to know
Carnac lies just off the Atlantic coast in southern Brittany. The Route de Alignments follows the course of the three main alignments, with car parks along the way. There's a visitor centre at the Alignements de Kermario (daily: May & June 9am–7pm; July & Aug 9am–8pm; Sept–April 10am–5.15pm; ⊛www.carnac.fr).

It's possible that the stones had some sort of ritual significance, linked to the numerous tombs and dolmens in the area; or they may have been the centre of a mind-blowing system to measure the precise movements of the moon – we simply don't know.

At the northwest end of the third and final alignment, Kerlescan, don't turn back as most visitors do. Keep walking to where the stones peter out in the thick, damp woodland of Petit Ménec, and the moss- and lichen-smothered menhirs seem even more enchanting, half hidden in the leaves. There's something incredibly stirring about these rows of megalithic monuments, and something mystical – it's that feeling you get when you walk into a quiet church, the sense of being in a spiritual place. And the knowledge that they were placed here for reasons we don't understand sends shivers down your spine.

Communing with Carnac's PREHISTORIC Past

25
Taking a trip up the EIFFEL TOWER

You catch glimpses of it all day as you stroll around the city: toytown-small from the Sacré-Coeur in the morning; pylon-sized as you saunter by the Seine after lunch; and looming omnipresent over the skyline as you linger over drinks in St Germain, trying to time your assault to coincide with the golden-pink dusk that everyone says provides the best backdrop to the views from the top. A short Metro ride and suddenly you're there. The excruciating wait in the throng underneath ticks away as you crane your neck to look up through the golden-lit tangle of metal and into the darkening sky, a perspective that enhances the tower's stature like no other can.

The smooth glide to the top is shared with reams of schoolchildren and camera-wielding fellow tourists, but they all seem to fade away as you step out of the packed lift and walk around the tower's four sides, the wind whistling past your ears and stinging your eyes into dampness.

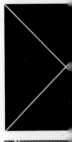

The city unfurls like a blanket below as you strain to distinguish less familiar landmarks nestling between the Louvre and the Champs-Elysées, and try to imagine the chic Parisian lives being played out behind the many lit windows.

On the hour, thousands of sodium lights fizz and pop all over the rusty-red metal, turning the tower into a crackling, lit-up version of itself. Locals and hardened travellers alike may scoff at the kitschy, magical lights, yet they seem to complete what remains the quintessential Parisian experience.

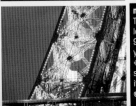

need to know
The tower is open daily (mid-June to Aug 9am–midnight, last entrance for top floor 11pm; Sept to mid-June 9.30am–11pm, last entrance for top floor 10.30pm), and you'll pay €11 to take the lift all the way to the top. It costs €11 to take the lift all the way to the top, €7.70 to the second floor and €4.20 to the first (€6/€4.20/€3.30 if you opt for the leg-wearying stairs). For more info, visit ⓦ www.tour-eiffel.fr.

25
Ultimate
experiences
France
miscellany

> *"France was a long despotism tempered by epigrams."*
>
> **Thomas Carlyle**

History

France takes its name from the **Franks**, a Germanic people who invaded the former Roman colony of Gaul in the fifth century. Clovis I (466–511) was the first Frankish king to unite what's now the core territory of modern France, though it wasn't until Charlemagne's empire was broken up in 843 that an independent **French kingdom** was created.

Louis XIV (1643–1715), the "Sun King", was France's longest-reigning, most extravagant and most absolute monarch. His grand palace at Versailles could accommodate 20,000 people in its 700 rooms, and though the exact figure is disputed, some estimates suggest it cost the current equivalent of a staggering US$300/£158 billion to build.

Though it saw Louis XVI to the guillotine in 1793 and ushered in the first of France's five republics, the **French Revolution** (1789–1799) wasn't quite the end of the monarchy: kings and emperors ruled France on four occasions in the nineteenth century. Though France currently has no king, it does have a claimant to the throne: a descendant of Louis-Philippe, the last King of France (1830–1848), Henri Philippe d'Orléans is ready to step in should the people tire of *la République*.

Santé!

France has been regarded as the world's premier **wine-producing** nation since English kings and nobles started buying up barrels of claret in the Middle Ages, but since the 1970s competition from upstart New World wines has challenged this monopoly. The rot began with the now notorious **Paris Wine Tasting** of 1976, when a blindfolded jury that included eight of France's top wine critics were horrified to discover they had chosen a Californian Chardonnay and Cabernet Sauvignon over the equivalent French wines. To the chagrin of the judges, some of whom refuse to discuss the tasting to this day, their verdict became known as the "Judgement of Paris", and has gone down in winemaking legend as the moment when the world realized that the French *terroir* wasn't the only soil capable of producing truly great wines.

"Never interrupt your enemy when he is making a mistake."

Napoleon Bonaparte

Napoléon complex

The man who called England "that nation of shopkeepers", **Napoléon Bonaparte** was born in Corsica in 1768 and became one of the greatest military commanders of all time, ruling France as Emperor between 1804 and 1814 and almost conquering the whole of Europe. Contrary to popular belief, his nickname, "le petit caporal", was not an allusion to his height, but an affectionate term – in fact, Napoleon was just over the average height for a Frenchman at the time, at 1.68m. He died in exile on St Helena in 1821, and was reburied in a vast mausoleum in Les Invalides, Paris, in 1840. Controversy continues as to what killed him; the original diagnosis was stomach cancer, but others claim he was poisoned with arsenic by an agent of the French royal family.

Haute cuisine

France is synonymous with gastronomic perfection, though some historians (and most Italians) claim that **haute cuisine** was introduced to the nation in the 1540s by Florence native Catherine de Medici, who brought a team of skilled chefs to Paris when she married Henri II. Whatever the truth, France had developed its own rich culinary tradition by the eighteenth century, blending regional styles with the lavish cuisine served at the royal court.

Today, gastronomic excellence is rewarded by **Michelin stars** (three being the highest), which were introduced in 1926 by way of the French tyre manufacturer's travel guides. According to Restaurant magazine, the country's top restaurants of 2006 are as follows:

Alain Ducasse at Plaza Athénée, Paris Modern French cooking from the only chef in the world with three Michelin stars in three different countries (France, the USA and Monaco).

L'Astrance, Paris Intimate split-level restaurant, serving contemporary, creative menus from chef Pascal Barbot.

Le Cinq, Paris Domain of chef Philippe Legendre, who creates sumptuous *haute cuisine* in the opulent surroundings of the *Four Seasons George V* hotel.

Michel Bras, Laguiole Deep in the Auvergne, blending minimalist Japanese presentation with traditional local specialities.

Pierre Gagnaire, Paris Modern and sophisticated decor to match modern, innovative (and very expensive) French cuisine.

Cuisine française?

Although **snails** (*escargot*) and **frog's legs** (*jambes* or *cuisses de la grenouille*) are often viewed as stereotypically French, *escargot* are usually served only during celebrations (and are a Catalan speciality), while frog's legs are more common fare in China, the Caribbean and Louisiana (USA). **French fries** (*pommes frites*) are thought to have originated in Belgium, but the "French" label probably dates from references made by Thomas Jefferson to the well-established French version he encountered during his period there as US ambassador (1785-89). One classic food that really is truly French is the **croissant**: it was first baked here in the mid-nineteenth century, although a modern recipe didn't appear until 1905, when the famous pastry was featured in a French-published cookery book. The oft quoted story that croissants were invented in Budapest or Vienna in the seventeenth century (during Turkish sieges) is pure myth.

France nucléaire

France's 59 **nuclear reactors** provide 75 percent of the country's energy, while its nuclear arsenal comprises an estimated 60 ASMP aircraft-based nuclear missiles and up to 288 submarine-based warheads. French **nuclear tests** in the South Pacific have often led to controversy. In 1985, French secret agents sank the Greenpeace ship *Rainbow Warrior* in Auckland harbour after it had been used to protest against tests at Mururoa Atoll, and a photographer was drowned trying to recover equipment. The incident caused a diplomatic row between France and New Zealand, but although the French government paid Greenpeace US$8.16m in compensation in 1987, full details of the bombing only came to light twenty years later, when it was revealed that French president François Mitterrand authorized the attack.

 # 7 Our Lady of Lourdes

Famed as the place where the Virgin Mary appeared to the 18-year-old Bernadette Soubirous in 1858, and as the source of spring water with supposed healing properties, **Lourdes** is by far the most important religious site in France. It's also one of the most revered places in the Roman Catholic world, attracting four to five million pilgrims annually – the small town contains around 270 hotels, second only to Paris.

 # 8 Merci pour fumer

Aromatic, full-strength and packing more tar than a four-lane *autoroute*, French cigarette brands **Gauloises** and **Gitanes** assumed iconic status after World War II, when they were very publicly puffed on by some of the nation's sexiest and most celebrated film stars, artists and philosophers. Despite the apparently vice-like grip smoking has on the French way of life, with over 40 percent of the total population (and alarmingly, 30 percent of doctors), taking a drag on a regular basis, the French government has finally declared war on the evil weed. As of February 1, 2007, smoking will be **banned** in most public places, and from January 1, 2008 (in line with almost every other European country) this will be extended to cover all bars and restaurants. Enforcing the ban, however, is likely to prove impossible, with most French smokers reacting to the news with a mixture of anger and bemusement – and with no intention to comply, despite hefty fines.

"The English, a spirited nation, claim the empire of the sea; the French, a calmer nation, claim that of the air."

Louis XVII

9 Cannes Cannes

Staged on the Côte d'Azur since 1939 and famed for its lavish post-screening parties, the glamorous, star-studded **Cannes Film Festival** has become one of the greatest showcases in the world for innovative, avant-garde movie-makers. Since 1955, the best film has received the **Palme d'Or** – awarded to French movies six times. But despite critical acclaim, and the fact that some 150–200 home-grown films are made here annually, the French movie industry has struggled commercially for years, its survival due more to government subsidies and tax breaks than commercial success.

▶▶ La France en filme – Gallic movie classics

The Return of Martin Guerre (1982). Set in sixteenth-century rural France, a soldier returns home after years at war, only to find his identity is questioned by his old friends, and even his wife. Remade by Hollywood as *Sommersby* in 1993.

Jean de Florette (1986). Charts the struggles of Jean, a hunchback, as he tries to work inherited land in southern France and battles the machinations of his wicked neighbours – he dies, but his daughter gets her revenge in the equally powerful sequel, *Manon des Sources* (1986).

Cyrano de Bergerac (1990). Richly lyrical tale of the sixteenth-century poet-cum-swordsman with the big nose, memorably portrayed by Gérard Depardieu. Cyrano reluctantly aids a young but dumb suitor to pursue the woman he actually loves but cannot have himself.

La Femme Nikita (1990). Cult hit and breakout movie for director Luc Besson, the tale of a delinquent woman who turns secret service agent.

Amélie (2001). Quirky romantic comedy starring Audrey Tautou, and based around Amélie's eccentric life in the Montmarte district of Paris.

10 Vive la France

France's most important festival (and national holiday) is **Bastille Day**, held every July 14 to commemorate the 1789 fall of the Bastille prison in Paris and the beginning of the French Revolution. Most French cities and towns organize firework displays and large balls on the evening of the 14th, but the main event is a large military parade held along the Champs-Élysées in Paris. Not everyone gets into the spirit, however: British Prime Minister Margaret Thatcher upset her French hosts in 1989 when she claimed, in reference to Bastille Day, that "all the French Revolution created was a pile of headless bodies with a dictator standing on top." Held every August at Trie-sur-Baise in the Midi-Pyrénées and drawing a loyal cult following, the French Pig-Squealing Championships is one of France's most bizarre "fetes folles", and sees participants act like pigs, competing on the basis of oinks, grunts and even, disturbingly, simulated suckling and mating.

11 The cycle of your life

Held each July, the Tour de France long-distance cycle race is the nation's biggest annual sporting event, with some 15 million people turning out to watch its riders streak past. Since it was established in 1903, it has been won by 36 French riders, more than any other nation – though Lance Armstrong of the US notched up a record seven victories, winning every single race between 1999 and 2005. Recent doping scandals (a whole team was implicated in 1998, and 2006 winner Floyd Landis returned a positive drugs test) have been portrayed as a "modern shame" on the race, but associations with intoxicants have been common throughout its history: in its early days, alcohol and drugs were used as a means of counteracting the punishing effects of long-distance cycling. In 1967, Englishman Tom Simpson died of heart failure on the notoriously strenuous Mont Ventoux during the 13th stage of the race – traces of amphetamines and alcohol were later found in his bloodstream.

"If you are lucky enough to have lived in Paris as a young man, then wherever you go for the rest of your life, it stays with you, for Paris is a moveable feast."

Ernest Hemingway

12 Literature

Thirteen French writers have won the Nobel Prize for literature – more than any other nation, and the country is justly proud of its rich literary heritage. A top ten of French novels might include:

Germinal, Émile Zola. Masterful depiction of the hardship endured by miners in northern France during the 1860s, and an early espousal of Socialist thought.

The Immoralist, André Gide. Powerful and shocking tale of sexual desire.

In Search of Lost Time, Marcel Proust. The lengthy seven-volume classic of modernist fiction, written as autobiography, tackling several weighty philosophical themes, most famously the role that memory plays in defining human character.

Madame Bovary, Gustave Flaubert. Flawlessly written tale of adultery that shocked the public in the 1850s.

Les Misérables, Victor Hugo. Popular novel that's latterly been made into an even more lauded musical, it follows the life of ex-convict Jean Valjean as he seeks meaning and forgiveness in nineteenth-century France.

The Outsider, Albert Camus. Only physical experience is real: Camus' hero lives, loves and murders apparently without emotion. As he waits for his execution, he concludes that the universe is totally indifferent to mankind.

La Père Goriot, Balzac. Follows the progress of an ambitious young law student as he becomes disillusioned with high society in early nineteenth-century France. Ends with the classic "It's between you and me now, Paris!"

Roads to Freedom, Jean-Paul Sartre. Sartre's thoughtful trilogy is regarded as his greatest work of fiction, an exploration of existential philosophy and the concept of freedom set against the background of 1930s France and World War II.

Second Sex, Simon de Beauvoir. The landmark book of twentieth-century feminism, largely autobiographical, arguing that society defines the male sex as normal or ideal, and women as aberrant or "the other".

Vagabond, Colette. Charts the life of a divorcee, circa 1910, as she works the music halls of Paris, struggling to gain the confidence to be truly independent, free of the confines of traditional male/female relationships.

"I have tried to lift France out of the mud. But she will return to her errors and vomitings. I cannot prevent the French from being French."
Charles de Gaulle

13 Eau de toilette

France has been the centre of the European **perfume** industry since the eighteenth century, and today, nine out of every ten French women use perfume while fifty percent of men use cologne. The grandmother of them all, **Chanel No.5** hit the shops in 1921, and has regularly topped sales charts since then. Myths abound as to why Coco Chanel chose the name, though it seems likely that she simply considered five her lucky number. Less credible is the story that No.5 was created by accident, when the final formula was unknowingly tampered with by a lowly assistant.

14 Beaux arts

With a roster of exceptional home-grown painters and sculptors and an equally impressive array of world-class galleries, France has a phenomenal **artistic heritage**. France began to eclipse Italy as the centre of the art world in the seventeenth century, when the work of Baroque painter Nicolas Poussin inspired a new wave of French artists. The Rococo school of the eighteenth century, Romanticism and Impressionism in the 1800s, and many of the twentieth century's post-Impressionist movements have also been dominated by French artists.

Bal au moulin de la Galette by Pierre-Auguste Renoir became the most expensive French painting to date in 1990, when Japanese businessman Ryoei Saito bought it for US$78m/£41m at Sotheby's New York – equivalent to around US$110m/£58m today. Taking the number two slot, Paul Cézanne's *Rideau, Cruchon et Compotier* fetched US$60.5m/£32m (US$70m/£37m today) at Sotheby's New York in 1999, the highest price ever paid for a still life – though it was later resold at a loss.

15 Great French inventions

France's most celebrated scientists are familiar worldwide: **Marie Curie** (1867–1934), who discovered radium (with husband Pierre) and pioneered research on radioactivity, remains the only person with a Nobel

Prize in both chemistry and physics; while **Louis Pasteur** (1822–1895) invented the process now known as pasteurization, as well as a vaccine for rabies. But French invention goes a lot further:

Bikinis Jacques Heim and Louis Reard are credited with inventing the skimpy bathing suit in 1946, naming it – appropriately enough given the excitement it caused – after Bikini Atoll in the Marshall Islands, site of the first US atom bomb test.

Braille Louis Braille (1809–1852) devised his system of reading for the blind in 1821.

Pencils Nicolas Conte developed the technology used to make pencils in 1795.

Sewing machines French tailor Barthelemy Thimonnier made the first sewing machine in 1830.

Scuba diving Emile Gagnan and Jacques Cousteau invented the first "aqualung" diving suit in 1943.

16 Personally speaking . . .

The oldest recorded human being (ignoring the Old Testament) was a Frenchwoman, one **Jeanne Louise Calment**, who was born in Arles in 1875 and died 122 years later in 1997. Apparently retaining a sense of humour, she is said to have remarked on her 120th birthday that "I've only got one wrinkle and I'm sitting on it".

According to French market research group IFOP, the most popular French personalities of 2005 were:

1 Zinedine Zidane, football player
2 Yannick Noah, tennis player
3 Nicolas Hulot, TV producer
4 Johnny Hallyday, singer
5 Jean Reno, actor

"Some people think luxury is the opposite of poverty. It is not. It is the opposite of vulgarity."
Coco Chanel

17 Little black dress

Launched in 1926 as part of her haute couture collection, Coco Chanel's **"little black dress"** did more to revolutionize the fashion world than almost any other garment. By the 1960s, the LBD had reached iconic status, mostly due to the series of chic Givenchy dresses worn by Audrey Hepburn in *Breakfast at Tiffany's* (1961) – one of which was sold by Christie's of London in December 2006 for a cool £467,200; the reserve price was £70,000.

> *"If French is no longer the language of a power, it can be the language of a counter power."*
> **Lionel Jospin**

18 Francophonie

French is spoken by around 150 million people around the world, though despite optimistic claims to the contrary by proud francophones, only 29 nations (not including overseas French territories) list French as a national language. La Francophonie is an organization dedicated to the promotion of French as an international language in opposition to English, and counts 53 states and governments worldwide as its members.

At least forty percent of modern English derives from the French language – the latter was the first language of the English nobility for almost 300 years after the Norman Conquest in 1066. Today, English is littered with French words and phrases, from double entendre to piece de résistance.

19 Fromage formidable

Cheese is a French obsession. More fromage is consumed here than in any other European nation, at 23kg per person per year, while France produces over 500 types of highly prized regional varieties, from Normandy's soft, creamy Camembert and Brie to Vieux Boulogne, an unpasteurized, beer-washed concoction that's widely held to be one of the smelliest in the world. The most expensive French cheese is truffle-stuffed Brie, which sells at around £45/US$85 per kilo, while the hardest is reputed to be Mimolette Extra

Vielle, with an outer shell as solid as a coconut. France is also the world's top producer of **goat's cheese**, with over 100 varieties, many of them sold in bizarre and highly memorable forms: Pouligny Saint Pierre comes in pyramids, while Sainte Maure de Touraine is sold in cylinders, each with a straw running through the middle as proof of authenticity.

20 Le Hip-Hop

French hip-hop emerged in the early 1980s, with DJs such as Dee Nasty, the "father" of French rap music and rapper **MC Solaar** becoming its most successful star – his first album *Qui sème le vent récolte le tempo* (1991) sold over 400,000 copies in France, and gradually gained him an international audience. With its roots in the relatively deprived African- and Arab-dominated suburbs – the *banlieues* – of cities such as Paris, Marseille, Lyon, Le Havre and LilleFrench rap has been the voice of the nation's marginalized communities for the last twenty years. Unlike British hip-hop, which has found it hard to compete with the vast array of US acts, the fluid, expressive nature of the French language has allowed rap to develop a unique identity in France.

21 French colonies

France was one of the great European **imperial powers** in the nineteenth century, second only to Britain in terms of territory controlled. France retains the largest empire of all the former colonial powers, though its remaining colonies (all ten of them) are now all overseas departments or communities of France. Four – French Guiana, Guadeloupe, Martinique and Réunion – have the same status as French *régions*.

22 Asterix the Gaul

The Gauls were a Celtic people who inhabited France long before the Roman conquest, and Brittany remains a Celtic stronghold today – as well as the home of **Asterix** and **Obelix**, much-loved fictional warriors and cartoon heroes who are supposed to have lived around 50 BC in the last village "of indomitable Gauls to hold out against the Roman invaders". The secret to the success of the village is the magic potion cooked up by druid Getafix, which provides superhuman strength, albeit temporarily – Obelix fell into the potion when young, making his super strength permanent.

Created in 1959 by René Goscinny and Albert Underzo, the series of 33 Asterix books has been translated into over 100 languages, while **Parc Astérix** (35km north of Paris) gets two million visitors annually – and makes a profit, unlike Disneyland Paris, which made a net loss in 2005.

23 Je t'aime

In 2004, condom-maker Durex confirmed one of the most enduring stereotypes of all time – that France is the home of the greatest **lovers** in the world. Polling some 350,000 participants from 41 countries, the survey found that on average, the French have sex 137 times a year – well above the global average of 103 – though only 32 percent claimed to experience an orgasm every time.

However, the 2005 survey saw the Greeks take the lead with a coronary-inducing 138 sex sessions per year, beating the French into a humiliating sixth place. And November 2006 saw a further blow to Gallic pride, when just 1,188 Parisian massed kissers failed to beat the record of 11,750 simultaneous snoggers achieved in Budapest in 2005.

"Man is condemned to be free."

Jean-Paul Sartre

24 Philosophy

France has produced some of the greatest thinkers in the history of philosophy, from Descartes and his seminal work on natural philosophy and geometry or Jean-Paul Sartre and the great existentialist thinkers of the Left Bank to post-modernists such as Michel Foucault.

▶▶ Great French philosophers

René Descartes (1596–1650). Best known for claiming "I think therefore I am", Descartes was a leading proponent of rationalism – using the rational mind rather than the unreliable senses to deduct scientific truth, as the empiricists advocated.

Blaise Pascal (1623–1662) Starting his career as a scientist, Pascal began the *Pensées* ("Thoughts"), after a religious epiphany in 1654, attacking Descartes' rationalism with Pascal's Wager – the concept that it is always better to believe in God, as the expected benefit from that belief is always greater than atheism.

Voltaire (1694–1778) Leading light of the French Enlightenment, and author of satires such as *Candide*, Voltaire is best known for his defence of religious freedom.

Jean-Paul Sarte (1905–1980) One of the founders of existentialism, but also lauded for his works of fiction and political activism, he refused the Nobel Prize for Literature in 1964 on the grounds that he had never accepted honours before, and did not want to be associated with establishment institutions.

Jacques Derrida (1930–2004) The founder of "deconstruction", a new insight into the meaning (or lack thereof) of words and texts, and regarded as one of the world's foremost modern philosophers.

25 Liberté, égalité, fraternité

Ever since the Revolution of 1789, France has been a hotbed of rebellion. The nineteenth century saw the July Revolution of 1830, the 1848 Revolution and the Socialist-inspired Paris Commune, which briefly controlled the city in 1871. Students continued the tradition in May 1968, when disagreements with university authorities led to violent clashes with the police and, eventually, a general strike by ten million workers. More recently, the riots in deprived French suburbs of autumn 2005 led to a state of emergency being declared, and eventually to tightened controls on immigration. Perhaps the most vociferous complainers of all, French farmers have proved notoriously recalcitrant protestors – blocking roads, smashing stockpiles of foreign imports and attacking branches of McDonald's in defence of their EU subsidies.

25 Ultimate experiences
France
small print

ROUGH GUIDES – don't just travel

We hope you've been inspired by the experiences in this book. To us, they sum up what makes France such an extraordinary and stimulating place to travel. There are 24 other books in the 25 Ultimate Experiences series, each conceived to whet your appetite for travel and for everything the world has to offer. As well as covering the globe, the 25s series also includes books on **Journeys, World Food, Adventure Travel, Places to Stay, Ethical Travel, Wildlife Adventures** and **Wonders of the World**.

When you start planning your trip, Rough Guides' new-look guides, maps and phrasebooks are the ultimate companions. For 25 years we've been refining what makes a good guidebook and we now include more colour photos and more information – on average 50% more pages – than any of our competitors. Just look for the sky-blue spines.

Rough Guides don't just travel – we also believe in getting the most out of life without a passport. Since the publication of the bestselling Rough Guides to **The Internet** and **World Music**, we've brought out a wide range of lively and authoritative guides on everything from **Climate Change** to **Hip-Hop**, from **MySpace** to **Film Noir** and from **The Brain** to **The Rolling Stones**.

Publishing information

Rough Guide 25 Ultimate experiences France Published May 2007 by Rough Guides Ltd, 80 Strand, London WC2R 0RL
345 Hudson St, 4th Floor,
New York, NY 10014, USA
14 Local Shopping Centre, Panchsheel Park, New Delhi 110017, India
Distributed by the Penguin Group
Penguin Books Ltd,
80 Strand, London WC2R 0RL
Penguin Group (USA)
375 Hudson Street, New York, NY 10014, USA
Penguin Group (Australia)
250 Camberwell Road, Camberwell, Victoria 3124, Australia
Penguin Books Canada Ltd,
10 Alcorn Avenue, Toronto, Ontario, Canada M4V 1E4
Penguin Group (NZ)
67 Apollo Drive, Mairangi Bay, Auckland 1310, New Zealand

Printed in China
© Rough Guides 2007
No part of this book may be reproduced in any form without permission from the publisher except for the quotation of brief passages in reviews.
80pp
A catalogue record for this book is available from the British Library
ISBN: 978-1-84353-820-2
The publishers and authors have done their best to ensure the accuracy and currency of all the information in **Rough Guide 25 Ultimate experiences France**, however, they can accept no responsibility for any loss, injury, or inconvenience sustained by any traveller as a result of information or advice contained in the guide.

1   3   5   7   9   8   6   4   2

Rough Guide credits

Editor: Polly Thomas
Design & picture research: Chloë Faram, Chloë Roberts
Cartography: Katie Lloyd-Jones, Maxine Repath

Cover design: Diana Jarvis, Chloë Roberts
Production: Aimee Hampson, Katherine Owers
Proofreader: Sarah Eno

The authors

James McConnachie (Experiences 1, 22) is author of the *Rough Guide to the Loire Valley*. **Helena Smith** (Experience 2) is a photographer and inveterate Francophile. **Ross Velton** (Experiences 3, 6, 8, 16, 23) has updated Rough Guides to *France*, and *Provence and the Côte d'Azur*. **Chris Straw** (Experience 4) lived and worked in France for several years. **Jan Dodd** (Experiences 5, 21) is author of the *Rough Guide to the Dordogne and the Lot*. **Ruth Blackmore** (Experiences 7, 15) is co-author of the *Rough Guide to Paris*. **Helen Marsden** (Experiences 9, 25) is a former Rough Guide editor and a big fan of the City of Light. **Neville Walker** (Experience 10) has updated Rough Guides to *France*, and *Provence and the Côte d'Azur*. **Stephen Keeling** (Experiences 11, 12, 14, 24, Miscellany) is a Rough Guide author and regular visitor to France. **Sarah Eno** (Experiences 13, 20) is a former updater of the *Let's Go Paris* guide. **James Smart** (Experience 17) is a keen snowboarder. **Kevin Fitzgerald** (Experience 18) has updated the *Rough Guide to France*.

Picture credits

Over 70 reference books and hundreds of travel
guides, maps & phrasebooks that cover the world

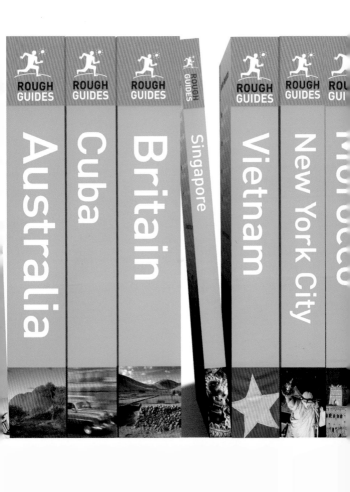

Index